The Grace
of an Eye

Poems

David Haskell Cohen

YONATY

To The All Merciful One, who inspires.

By the same author:

Chosen People
and other poems

Angels, Snakes and Ladders
Memoirs of a Jew from British India

Yonaty Publishing
12/13 Shalom Bonayich
Netivot 87804
Israel
(+972) 08 994 4095

Distributed in the UK by:
M. Shaw
8 Moundfield Road
London N16 6DT

First published 2000
Reprinted 2002

A catalogue record for this book is available
from the British Library

ISBN 965 90386 1 5

Designed by Jonathan Cohen

Printed in Israel

Prefatory Note

David Haskell Cohen was born in Calcutta in 1925, and educated at St Xavier's College—all papers set and examined at Cambridge University.

His first poem, *Reading*, was written at the age of sixteen. Another early poem, *If I Could,* appeared in *The Times Illustrated Weekly of India* in 1949.

He believes with Goethe and the classical English poets that the best poetry is written within the disciplines of metre and rhyme, and with Robert Frost that writing "free verse" is "like playing tennis with the net down".

A political and foreign news correspondent and columnist for many years, he later became creative director and owner of an advertising agency in London's Mayfair. He now lives with his wife in Jerusalem, near two of his sons, their wives and his many grandchildren. His third and youngest son lives with his wife and children in the US. All three sons are Orthodox Rabbis.

The poems here fall roughly into two groups: those written during his youth in India (*Earlier Poems*), and those written after his retirement and immigration to Israel.

His memoirs, *Angels, Snakes and Ladders,* and a second anthology, *Chosen People and other poems*, are also published by Yonaty.

Contents

Indian rain

What is that sound I hear once more
What scent of heavy rain?
The flooding street, the taxi horn
The weeping window pane.

And then those last few weighty drops
That shake a waiting leaf
As silver coins on beggar's hand
Of wet and tattered grief.

Falling into my heart again
Whatever can it mean?
The scent and sound of Indian rain
When I was seventeen.

2000

The cherubim

In Temple times two figures made
Of beaten gold with outstretched wings
Above the Ark when Israel prayed
Their wings entwined like loving things

One morning I, as one of two
Cohanim, turned upon the dais
With hands in blessing as we do
God's bidding from the holy place

I know not what took hold of me
My flesh transformed to hammered gold
As for one flashing moment we
Became the cherubim of old.

Purple blossoms

I saw a line of purple blossoms lying
Along a city roadside drain
And there were golden petals sighing
Shaken down by wind and rain –
Surely hints which heaven ever flings
Upon our laboured, dowdy, man-made things.

Heaven's not just in roses, grapes and trees
But in human and non-human faces
The dimly wondering look of chimpanzees
And all immense and open places –
I have seen souls walking whom I recognise
And sadly have to lower my longing eyes.

Heaven is all around; they call it Nature
To bring it down to a man-manageable stature.

He

He made me with a weakness at the core
And so most things that I was yearning for
Could not be realised on earth; I cried
The all-around-me youthful joy denied –

He ordered me to sing, filled me with love
Then threw me down from fields of dreams above
He let me go, I wandered from his tent
And then he drew me back and said "Repent"

As father plays with son he tested me
He gave me gifts and he protected me
The world saw I was blessed and wondered why
Of what high worth was simple stricken I?

Mine is the offering most beloved of Man
A poor one's broken pieces in a pan.

You cried

You saw the broken people and you cried
Coming from affluence, to such horrors blind
And hearing you, how to explain my joy
At simple human pity for humankind
Unless came wondrous thought that this was true –
In grief and gladness God was sobbing too.

Sheet music

They gave me a piece
Of sheet music today
My heartbeat's not right
So the hospital say

Can't say I'm surprised
After all the rough use
Wild plucking of strings
Heavy thumping of blues

My Lord you have filled
The world with such art
The hints of your presence
Have shaken my heart.

So late

My Love, my Love, why are you so late?
It must be past the hour, long gone the date –
The moon with beams searches the luckless sky
The staring sun still glowers with red-hot eye

No sign! It is so long since there was word –
The scroll is read out loud, the promise heard
But where the table stood and the light shone
Now there is darkness and the bread has gone

Our house is broken, still I near-broken wait
Outside the waiting wall where there's no gate –

My Lord, my Lord, why are you so late?

Israel's summer

When Israel wears her summer suit
Trees show udders of sweet brown fruit
And under skies of deep blue silk
Goats bear veined white melons of milk

And turtle doves make throaty songs
The sea froths in where the beach belongs
Balconies hang big purple blooms
And blinds come down on shady rooms

Through the jewelled dark, cool breezes blow
Cloudless skies stage a lunar show
The nights are full of bright surprises
The moon's in various shapes and sizes

But life's not sweet on the city street
Where car horns bleat in the pressing heat
There's a concentration on grab and lust
And the mindless urge of beat or bust

We are the people of the heavenly book
And all the nations come and look
The Western Wall is rent with prayer
What cries are hidden in the crevices there!

Yet God-forsaking parties boast
Of who can defy high heaven the most
The smoke-filled hate gets in your eyes
Like kerosene fumes of barbecue fries.

A nation like any other? No chance!
We're cursed or blessed by the circumstance
Of being special. How else survived?
How else at this high point arrived?

Let summer speak, rich earth relate
This people's coming wondrous state
See heaven's windows flung apart
Upon the turn of Israel's heart.

Screaming in Jerusalem

Among the hills of God
And under David's star
The ambulances scream
With bodies from a car
Mangled in a crash
And deaf-determined death-defying dash

Frustrated taxis hoot
And car alarms declaim
Hee-hawing donkey laughs,
Loud voice of doom proclaims
News of death's latest count
Another burial on the overcrowded mount

The knives that stabbed the Jews
In stabs that never cease
Now turn to cut Jerusalem
In pieces in place of peace -
There's weeping from the sky
The prayed-for rains at last are coming by

In pairs the silent doves
Heads bowing as they go,
As though whole city were
A synagogue, are so
Worried and perplexed,
Wondering what is going to happen next

Among the hills of God
Death's angel once before
Halted when David bought
Araunah's threshing floor
And built an altar there –
Oh answer, too, dear Lord, our sacrificial prayer.

Tell me

Tell me you love me
I'll say it too
Cling to me, sing to me
I'll cling to you

Met you it seems so
Often before
Only in dreams though
No more, no more

Hearing no word, no
Answering song
Like a lost bird
All life long

Holocaust memorial

I dreamed a line of stern clean-shaven men
Striding like soldiers looking straight ahead,
Passed, old and young, to a cavernous den
A ghostly march of killers long since dead –
While watching all around upon earth's plain
The solemn faces of the bereaved and slain.

Beneath the earth I went and saw the rock
Was shaped like grinning skulls with pointed teeth
Who wins, who loses, see the murderers mock
The murdered from the very ground beneath.
We shall not rest till we have testament
A guilt-enshrining marble monument.

These tongue-tied stones for centuries shall relate
Who murdered whom in cold undying hate.

See what ship

See what ship comes creaking into port
Hold crammed and timbers bending
Her time has come to bear but who had thought
Such treasures she was tending
Beams of cedar, tons of gold,
Oil and spices, wine grown old,
These bounties from her many merits wrought
Now cast upon the shore of her days ending.

About her neck richer than rubies twined
The arms of children's children are caressing
Let tears fall like pearls upon her blessing
Fast changing into treasures of a different kind.

1998

Land

What land is this that needs men's blood to thrive
And constant war and mutilating shells?
Across the world for land, more land, they strive
Making their business individual hells

And here in God's own promised land, what pain
For war, more war, has ever been decreed
Drive out the Canaanites, and then again
Under new enemies and by new knives we bleed

All land is battle ground must we believe?
And how on earth are we to understand
That earth was made for us to war and grieve
And take by force and hold as burial land

Yet, all the land is Mine, the Lord has said –
For living surely, not just for the dead.

The Prince

I have known your face it seems
In sleep that runs deeper than dreams –
We have walked by softly lapping seas
Talked in long grasses under spreading trees
Lived in each others eyes and caught
The quick beginnings of a thought
In one another. Yet now you pass me by
With blank, uncomprehending eye.

It is I who am to blame,
I cannot even remember your name
Cannot call out from this wrapping I'm in
This old chrysalis skin –
Ah! If only I could snake out
I would laugh, shake out
My golden hair
And take the air
With Prince or Princess.

I would be your country
Occupy me!
My pale blue skies
Are alive with songbirds, my fields
With fruit and flower, my ways
Of happy laughter.

But I see I am too late, your eyes
Have found another.
I am out of my time
In this night of falling dreams –
You must go where you will and I
Have still to journey far
Under an unfamiliar sky
Afire with desire –
Moth for star.

Moving at seventy

Finding an apartment
In Jerusalem is hard these days.
Prices are high, and then
As grandparents you need space
For visiting children.
Good apartments, we're told, have a "view".
Seen from the hillside of Bayit Vegan
A panorama of glittering lights of the city.
Some favour facing south,
We like to face towards the Temple.

Moving's more painful when you're older,
New immigrants but over seventy
We couldn't come earlier.
Now we have to wait months
To move in to our new apartment
And then we don't know how long we've got
Before having to move again,
If you see what we mean.

We'll be taken to a lower floor, of course,
And accommodation will be strictly limited.
But we're hoping with all our souls
That we'll have a view.

1997

A new grandson

Sing! And make tremble the end of that word
Sing! And give praises unto the Affeared
Winter has yielded a skyful of sun
A new grandson is born and downhill I run
To be caught in picture at hospital room
In slow yellowing light of glad afternoon.

1997

Age

Age brings its own
Especial pain
We feel the slowing
Of the train
The unfamiliar
Expectation
Of being put off
At the next station
With all our longings
Still unpacked
And left upon
The luggage rack

Or on one oddly
Troubled night
A lovely
Long forgotten sight
Comes like an
Uninvited thing
Puts out its hands
And starts to wring
An old man's heart.

Early Poems

Reading

I read the poet knowing
The greatest poetry consists
Of thoughts and feelings
That can themselves be expanded into poems.
Yet I feel a great outpouring of spirit
A dimming and dropping
Into depths of subconsciousness
As if this were the only
The breaking reality.

I am lost amid the spirit
Without identity or personal feeling
Only the message the poet chose
Like the glance of an eye
Like a lisp of the lip
I am lost in the eternity of its meaning

1941

Bengal 1943

See mother on your shrunken breast
I lay my head
This grey, this black, this shining street
Burns to the stomach, you said.

See mother on your withered arm
I hang my hand
I draw it slowly to the cold
Knuckled wrist band

See mother to your ringed ribs
I press my ear
I sense the swift-stilled void, the hollowness
Lightning fork of my fear

See mother, mother how the wind
Plays with your hair
Drawing it round about your face
In moving curve, in smiling grace
Caresses the bony brow, mourns, cries
Before the breathless horror of your round, your
staring eyes.

1943

What shall we do with these dead men?

What shall we do with these dead men, let them rot?
Only the shrieking of birds, only the hot
Silence of Bengal sun upon rags and bones
Unburied yet though buried were their groans

Shall these bones live? A quiet voice inquires
As murmurs and rumbles come, and earth expires
Mouthfuls of dead, rocks tumble from the sky
A roar comes riding on a hurricane and I

In terror see the armies of the dead
Marching with fearful Vengeance at their head –
Where are the murderers hidden – what oh what
Shall we do with these dead men, let them rot?

1947/2000

Chorus at the Red Sea

FROM "MOSES" THE PLAY, 1946

So let us bare our hearts and sing
The praises of the Lord
With every bird
Our joy takes wing
To dart among the parting
Clouds with dreams as yet unheard
So let us sing
So let us bare our hearts and sing
The praises of the Lord.

With one fell roar
The waters bore
Our swift deliverance
And not a ripple now
Upon the sea
Our people free.

With one great stroke
The back He broke
Of all our slavery
His mighty hand
Was felt as land
Appeared beneath our feet

Amazingly
A pathway in the sea.

So let us bare our hearts and sing
The praises of the Lord
With every bird
Our joy takes wing
To dart among the parting
Clouds with dreams as yet unheard
So let us sing
So let us bare our hearts and sing
The praises of the Lord.

At Pharoah's Palace

FROM "MOSES" THE PLAY, 1946

PHAROAH:
I do not know your God, what is his name?
Ask any of my people who is Ra
And they will show you, burning bright above
The Sun, the giver-out of light and heat;

27

Ask any of my people who is Noot
And they will show you, blue and grey and red,
The changing colours of the sky. And can
You show to us the nature of your God?

MOSES:
Signs will not be wanting if you refuse
To let our people go. With fire and sword
The Lord will manifest Himself on all His enemies.
You ask His Name and yet you will not understand
The Name I speak to you. It is *I Am That I Am.*
Who was before the earliest chime of time
Before the stars He jewelled in the sky
Before the rays of the all-warming sun
Swaddled the fresh-formed body of the earth;
Who is in all things great and all things small
In every living thing; and will be when the sun
Has lost his fire and dies of burning cold.
And now this God of all has come to be
The spirit of our people, and the words
That from my lips now fall are weighted words
Words weighted with the passion of the Lord.

Falling down

And must our eyes forever roam
Forever scour the earth?
Or must our lips forever burn
And never turn to mirth?
No, no, the silver hands of dawn
Will bring our love to birth.

And must the birds of sorrow ever
Heavy laden fly?
Or must all dreamers and all dreams
Forever fret and die?
No, no, for giants will rise by night
And break the darkening sky.

Ah yes the earth will come to birth
And children tease the sun
And cities will rise and startle the skies
And the whole world will be one.
Oh yes these days will be buried deep
When our great fight is done.

Gather the trumpets, sound the drums
Let the voice of the people sing
Round and round the crumbling walls
Seven times let the trumpets ring
Jericho's falling, falling down
War and hunger and suffering.

1949

If I could

If I could I would shake this world of wire and stone
See it come crashing rather than Love should die
Having no place to stretch its branches in.

They say they will remake Man but I hope they will
     not forget
To put the eyes in his face and a song in his heart
And a dream in his head

So that he can lift his arms to the stars and not be
Tangled in by wire, suffocated by stone
Lost in a glittering city, having a song unsung.

1951

30

My son

What will he be when he grows up?
Defend him
From the khaki men and the men in grey
From the dinner on Sunday and snooze men;
Let him get a profession but save him
From the snake-eyed men, the hard secret rulers
In the unnoticed building without a nameplate.

And yet, barrister or businessman,
It is all the same
Taught to think he will be appalled
At the awful burdensome boredom of it all
Where sunset and entrancing sea
Sing only of lost islands where men become beasts
And one has to turn back and there is
No edge to the earth.

And yet I would not have him different
Let him sail
On the great tides of illusion and the wine-dark sea
And come back half-bald and a little grey
But singing with a deeper throated defiance
Knowing the swaying rivers under the sea.

1959

Song of a shirt

When all his words are crumpled linen
And all his aspirations stale
In the perspiration of unfruitful endeavour
Then lay the man out for a tumble wash
And an iron and press under the soil.

But set the iron to gentle for a silken soul
Do collar and cuffs with care
And let him go pearl buttons gleaming
Folded and fresh in his blue hue starch
Wrapped in a nylon envelope to heaven.

CHORUS:
Unstitch each painful hem
Unsew each aching button
Unweave the worn-out cotton
Until in miraculous metamorphosis
Shirt returns to cotton bolls
In some sun plantation land
Swaying in the humming air
White on the seed.

1961

Memorandum

In the office uselessly making
Memos dead in a hundred years
    The sale of this to those
    And that to these
Can't we go out to the large lands of our birth
Return to the earth?

No, for now all is wall enclosed
Those large lands where we walked and talked
    Typewriters clicking
    And clocks ticking
Executive armies, director-administered
It's a small world.

1959

Ruthless

Suddenly we became ruthless
Clutched the rose
Snatched at the lily
Scrabbled for gold, wine, songs
Sunlight, desire
Thrust flint-hard hands
Into the stream in vain –
Through brittle fingers
The waters of life escaped,
The flowers wilted
The sunlight faded
And only the fever
Burning the flesh
Remained.

Now truth comes like sea breeze and birdsong
That only he with hands as tender
Fingers as pliant
As stems of kindliness –
Only that madman with a dream in his eyes
Can hold, can have
Life to live, Love to love.

1956

Reflection

His cold north room looked out
On a grey street, and soon
He pitied himself, and longed
For the bright sun. Then suddenly
One unexpected afternoon, that sun
Burst its reflection on a window pane.
He saw it from where he sat
Wondering the ways God takes to reach to Man.

1957

The dead embroiderer's house

Alone in the dark room
Suddenly there is a scent of oranges
Growing pungent
As varnished wood rotted with worms.
I see where you've gone
Among oranges of velvet
Sweet kumquats and lemons made of silk.
Around you the tigers are only painted
And elephants are still just a wild idea.

1976

Who are you? Where are you from?

Aaron, all his holy linen
Spattered with a he-goat's blood
From him taking a beginning
Through the kings and chronicles
Standing sceptred, hands in blessing
While the Roman armies gathered
While the pillage raged and razed
And the smell of burning incense
Mixed with smell of burning babes.

Led into captivity
Across the Babylonian river
Hung our harps upon the willows
Cut our thumbs, we would not play.
Then arose the great yeshivas
Yavneh, Sura, Pumbeditha,
A thousand Sages crossing, countering
Wove the Babylon Talmud.

When Ezekiel left with many
Stayed behind in Babylon
Princely favourites, spoiled and pampered
Lolling in mid-Eastern sun
Eating melons, gossiping
Left behind by history
Trading with the gutteral merchants
Far from ships and salt and sea.

Drifting westwards to Aleppo
Bargaining in old Baghdad
Then the hard-faced Turk oppression
Gave the urge to flee away,
Hearing rumours, unrest spreading
Marketplaces seethe with trouble
Knives are glinting, minarets
Call to holy war their followers.

Now the passage through the mountains
Eastwards to the luscious valleys
Past the frontier tribesmen's rifles
Past the carrot-haired effendis
Paused where Alexander halted
In the shade of peach and pear trees
By the bearded Guru's temple
By the five exalted rivers.

"Come", the letters urged, "more eastward",
Come across the Indian desert
To the hot and steaming city
On the banks of the brown Hooghly
Where the sun sets on the Empire
Where the topeed men play polo
And the mills of England slowly
Grind the wealth of India.

Here the carriages are drawing
Ladies to the Eden Gardens
Here the gentlemen are sipping
Whiskies in the sunset club –
Coolies pull the coir fanning
Bearers swat the battening flies
On the pavements cows are brooding
Vendors call, stars shine and beggars die.

Drink the cans of proffered milk
Eat the sweetmeats of the East
Kill the fatted fowls and roast
Golden as the crisp potatoes,
Fill the jars of salted tidbits
Pickling on the sunny ledges –
Paunchy fathers with their sons
Proudly go to synagogue.

Holy are the candelabra
Blazing like Aladdin's cave
Velvet are the prayer cases
Gloriously the baritones
Of the minister resound
Round the starred and vaulted ceiling
While the ladies' silks and satins
Rustle in the balconies.

No, I will not let you rest yet
Up and take your beds and bolsters
Go before the storm breaks over
England's brightest jewel ever
A thousand die before a bread shop
Flies are gathering, vultures sit
Guns of an insurgent navy
Pound upon the western shore.

Now begins the travel outward
London, New York, Sydney, Cape Town,
See the wandering Jews disperse
In their heads the dreams they cannot
Quite recall, the blood red sunsets,
Faces crowding by the million
And the strange, dust-swirled excitement
Of the gathering monsoon.

"Who are you?" they ask us puzzling
In the primly patterned suburb –
We with eyes unseeing whisper
Mumble incoherently
Seeing and not seeing rivers,
Seas and trees and centuries
Rocks and roads and far-off cities
Hopes and gladnesses and pities.

1960

Nightmare

The bullets a Sheriff fired in a Western
Hit three babies in a paddy field.
The bandits gunning in a New York alley
March to a royal palace in Accra
The politicians play a Whitehall farce
Men grin and cripples falter in the grass.
We are now closing down, closing down, pet
Switch off, switch off, switch off your set.

The chariot wheels that thunder in the film
Grind down a grovelling peasant in Peru
The strangler lurking in an English moor
Assaults a child in far-off India.
Beethoven's music underscores the crime
Our guilt goes wave on wave through space and time.
We are now closing down, closing down, pet
Switch off, switch off, switch off your set.

But we can't switch off, switch off our set.

1961

Those who dream

Those who dream and those who doubt
Search for Truth and find Love out
Wander in the highest hills
Struggle in the darkest mills
They will see at last the proof
Growing on Heaven's fallen roof.

Let the merchants of the squares
Buy and sell their stocks and shares
Let the politicians scheme
Pay a slogan for a dream –
Only Love and tears will bind
The bricks of a new humankind.

All that's built on power must
In the end return to dust
All the steel and all the stone
Are not worth a woman's moan
All the armies, all the ships
Are nothing to a poet's lips.

When you lay the concrete track
Know the grass will find a crack
To grow, the gentle rose will lift
A scented head, and slow or swift,
All tyrants go, wrong or right,
As fleeting as a meteorite.

Those who dream and those who dare,
Trees with fireflies in their hair,
Those who weep and those who toil
Will conquer with a single smile,
Those to whom the world belongs
Will win it back with burning songs.

1957

Last train

All the people in the Underground train were tired
All the names of the stations were fuddled with sleep
All the days of the year rattled and rolled
Everyone travelled from nowhere to nowhere.

1963

Tired

He was tired of eating
And tired of sleeping
Tired of dressing and undressing
And never could he review his life
As sunset from a hill
Or break beyond the rhythm and be still.

1963

Pearly dreams

In the small box that is my head
My pearly dreams a-dreaming lie
As when at din of day or dead
Of night, one lone and lidless eye
Unsleeping from its very birth
Turns in wonder from heaven to earth.

1996

Love

Hearing the singing I drew near
The crowds upon the mountain pressed
The evening flaring like my breast
Madly on running feet till fear
Then terror lifting me I saw you clear.

And straight the dusk was there
Upon the pavement you and I
Were face to face, I wondered where
The crowds, the singing and the mountain high
Had fled, stifling my every cry.

1957